URBAN
REFLECTIONS

ILLUSTRATED WORLD CITIES

URBAN
REFLECTIONS
ILLUSTRATED WORLD CITIES

HAROLD LINTON

ILLUSTRATIONS BY RICHARD ROCHON

Published in Australia in 2004 by
The Images Publishing Group Pty Ltd
ABN 89 059 734 431
6 Bastow Place, Mulgrave, Victoria, 3170, Australia
Telephone: +61 3 9561 5544 Facsimile: +61 3 9561 4860
Email: books@images.com.au
Website: www.imagespublishinggroup.com

Copyright © The Images Publishing Group Pty Ltd 2004
The Images Publishing Group Reference Number: 570

National Library of Australia
Cataloguing-in-Publication entry:

Linton, Harold
Urban reflections: illustrated world cities.

ISBN 1 876907 99 1.

1. Architectural drawing. 2. Cities and towns in art.
I. Rochon, Richard. II. Title

720.222

Designed by The Graphic Image Studio Pty Ltd, Mulgrave, Australia
Website: www.tgis.com.au

Film by Mission Productions Limited
Printed by Everbest Printing Co., Ltd. in Hong Kong/China

IMAGES has included on its website a page for special notices in relation to this and our other publications.
Please visit this site: www.imagespublishinggroup.com

Dedication:

to Jerome

to Joel

to Paul

to Martin

to Theresa

to Annette

to Caramarie

CONTENTS

FOREWORD

Since the emergence of conscious design, nascent architects have needed to invent methods to document their ideas, as tools to explore options within the design process, and to explain their concepts to others. Over time, the evolution of techniques has stretched from primitive trial-and-error constructions to sophisticated computer animations. But at the very heart of the craft of architecture has always existed the art of drawing.

The language of this art is as varied as the spoken word. At the most personal level, each designer creates his own system of markings that becomes an efficient method of exploring a concept and documenting its development for his own use. Although sometimes being in themselves objects of high artistic quality or historical documents of great research value, these drawings are created for the architect's own enlightenment as part of his process of discovery, much as a composer might employ his personal version of notation to record his musical thoughts.

At a more public level, the skill of architectural rendering is used as a method of enabling others to understand just what the designer is proposing, and to persuade them to approve or even champion the concept, or to fund the construction budget. The refinement and accuracy required for these purposes are critical, and while the task is rarely done for the education of the architect at the point at which these drawings are usually prepared, the result can sometimes also be enormously instructive to him.

It is unusual that an architect has the skill or the time to produce this latter form of drawing. He will turn to a professional, of which there are many, who has the technical qualifications to achieve the required results. But when the delineator, of which there are few, is able to transcend mere skill and bring the work to the aesthetic level that Richard Rochon practices, the result can often become an artistic end in itself.

I have had the great good fortune of collaborating (for that is the ultimate relationship of architect and illustrator) with Richard Rochon for the past 20 years, and the results of his talent are well documented herein. His work has certainly been instructive to me and invaluable to the success of the projects depicted. But much more, his artistry has also brought understanding and delight, and for that I am most grateful.

David M. Childs
Skidmore, Owings & Merrill

PREFACE

The impact of the built environment on human daily life and on the natural environment is a prominent issue in today's public discourse, and is often the subject of acrimonious debate.

It was not always so. There was a time when the addition of infrastructure to open land and buildings to towns and cities was welcomed. Parkways, bridges, rows of townhouses, department stores, government buildings and college campuses stand in testimony to successful human embellishment of countryside and city at a time of little or no public conversation about their initiative or production. The drawings of that time were technically descriptive, a reflection of the designers' skill and the public's trust, intended to facilitate implementation rather than communicate with an audience.

The drawings in this book are of a time that requires communication about building design to a large audience. The citizenry, in an endless variety of forums, now holds sway over the process of design and building, always it seems, desperate to hold back the forces of evil that are about to destroy a beautiful place. These drawings reflect their role to depict, to educate, and to facilitate the discussion.

A contemporary rendering must show truthfully the dimension and composition of a place and its intended character. A computer-aided photographic image may be more precise, and technologically more appropriate, but it leaves little to the realm of possibility. The drawing invites its viewer to partake in the optimism of possibility and even desire. The hand-drawn image can suggest that one lingers, to consider its elements and imagine oneself in the scene. Longer examination can illuminate what it is about a place that makes it appealing, how one might feel walking there, and how that place might contribute to one's daily life in a particular town or city.

Richard Rochon's drawings, in concert with Harold Linton's editing and the contributing ideas of an illustrious host of architects, extend an invitation to their audience to linger among the acknowledged great places of our world. The drawings themselves are artifacts of great skill and bear attention to the challenge they set for their author, and for his performance in response. Their collection together here is additionally a resource of reference for students of city design, be they professionals or citizens.

Rochon's rendered compendium of great urban places across history reminds us of the human capacity for timeless creation. These drawings present themselves in service to enlighten the discussion of design and the public realm, and in so doing they are a civic resource that has the power to guide the building of cities in our time and into the future.

Elizabeth Plater-Zyberk, FAIA
Dean, University of Miami School of Architecture
April, 2003

INTRODUCTION

Architectural illustrations are among the earliest visual evidence for the dreams of public spaces. They serve as a preview of the plans for dynamic urban change and of the myriad ways in which successful design projects in architecture, interior design, urban planning, and landscape architecture are realized or are yet to be realized. In discussing the urban design experience that follows, the focus is on the illustrator. The essence of sketching the urban concept lies in the discovery of pictorial ideas that integrate the illustrator's imagination and analysis with the architect's vision of place. In conversations with the architect and design team, the illustrator probes for information that will unlock the creative initiative to yield an image that captures the essence of the architecture and the imagination of the public. The basis of the unique relationship between Richard Rochon and architects throughout the world is his uncanny ability to capture the metaphor.

Urban Reflections: Illustrated World Cities takes you on a dynamic illustrative walking tour through world cities—one that illuminates the diversity and distinctive urban places where local materials are used to express the unique qualities of dwelling places, shops, town squares, and the vernacular environment. An urban explorer sees the high-rise towers, office buildings, apartments, and commercial spaces that permeate our urban centers. Streets and parks offer brief encounters of a personal nature with urban dwellers, and with the act of coming together either facilitated or inhibited by design, enables us to experience the presence of others and ponder the experiences and feelings made possible by a flourishing urban life.

Urban Reflections: Illustrated World Cities is composed of five parts—North American Urbanism, Southern Hemisphere Transformations, Mediterranean Light, Asia–Pacific Emergence, and European Traditions. It explores the symbiotic relationship between the art of architectural illustration and aesthetic

achievements of urban architecture, supported by thought-provoking commentary of world-renowned urban spaces from leading international architects and design professionals. Included in this illustrative survey of the fabric and texture of urban life are the elements of urban architecture—lights, signs, benches, trees, buses, trains, monuments, neighborhoods, low- and high-rise office buildings and residences, and of course people, captured with the activity of the street. The fully representative illustrations of contemporary urban planning and city spaces, as well as the artist's response to icons of the history of architectural achievements in urban design, portray the differences and similarities of the world's cities—the differences in dress and culture, and the similarities of street activities of people meeting and greeting, shopping, working, playing and relaxing.

Structures fulfill our needs. It is our habitation within and around them, however, which brings them to life, adding the significance of place to our culture and history. The impact of a sense of place is a point in a world whose setting, scale, and natural context reflect the urban experience of intimacy and surprise. The most adept at illustrating these environments are attuned to capturing significant attributes of the design concept. By making mental notes of visual information, the mind is used almost like a camera to make snapshots of specific details as well as broader, more expansive information. The illustrator distills the essence of information, including all the conditions and contradictions necessary to understand the physical design, including lighting, material texture, color, scale, site and location, space, and architectural form.

The illustrations in this book are, of course, a limited selection of urban life and architecture designed by world-renowned architects and urban planners. I can make no claim that this book is either complete or even truly representative. However, the architecture and urban spaces shown here are those that leading architects and educators believe to be distinctive and worthy of being shown in this collection, and I believe there are many lessons to be learned from them. During this period of a renewed sensibility to the quality of urban life, we offer this collection in support of what has been true in architecture throughout the ages, that the design of urban space is first and foremost for the benefit of people. Secondly, contemporary urban architecture and planning must consider all of those human factors and lessons from the past that influence our positive experience and the enjoyment of place.

For over four decades, the architectural illustrations of Richard Rochon have provided a body of visual evidence of the design and growth of the urban environment around the world. Rochon's illustrations have captured significant architectural projects including multi-story office towers, inner harbor developments, and new urban parks. His architectural illustrations have focused attention, increased public interest, and rallied support for the preservation and rehabilitation of our architectural heritage. Underlying the vision of his work is the artistic sensibility to animate and make real the life and zest of urban space.

Also included in this book is a selection of the images produced during the illustration process: visual note-taking, studies in line, tone, and texture, compositional studies and refinements. These preliminaries offer an especially revealing look at the translation of the urban design concept into the earliest visualizations that often result in provocative images of significant appeal and support. Their fine and seemingly effortless instrumentation reflects the confidence of an artist in spontaneously composing elegant pictorial design. They reveal the essence of urban architecture, which comprises shaping space and lending human character to the environment, while at the same time reflect successful examples of urban places that retain the vitality for which they were designed.

Harold Linton

ABOUT RICHARD ROCHON

Drawing, in its various forms and media, plays an integral role in the architectural design process. Much has been written about this process by well-known contemporary and historical members of the design professions, addressing the many avenues of communication: the generative sketch, with which design concepts are conceived and communicated; the preparation of study sketches and drawings, which act to refine and unify an idea during its evolution; and finally the representative drawing, which attempts to accurately communicate the design intention.

In the discussion of drawing for architecture and urban design that follows, the focus is on the representative drawing and the special skills of the illustrator in capturing pictorial ideas as they occur throughout the various phases of the architectural design process. Richard Rochon's vision in this creative process originates with a search for composition and a deftness to plan the manner in which eye movement will find the center of interest in the illustration. Rochon's ability to uncover the illustrative scheme appears magical, but in reality, it originates with the discipline of repeated practice in drawing and painting.

Included throughout the book is a broad sampling of images produced during the architectural design process and many drawings produced from observation and analysis. Many of these drawings were based on quick spontaneous sketches produced on-site or from photographic documentation of the subject returned to the office for analysis and elaboration. These fine and seemingly effortless illustrations reflect the confidence of the artist in spontaneously composing elegant pictorial design—a compositional ability that unlocks the natural beauty of the subject as it simultaneously and often spontaneously reveals the essence of architecture and urban design. Rochon's art of composing pictorial space for illustrations of significant historic and contemporary architecture lies in his passion for design and in the study of abstraction and representation in drawing, painting, and architectural design.

Though Rochon aspired to be an architect, he applied his talents primarily to visualization and architectural delineation. Working in a variety of media—oil, transparent watercolor, acrylic, gouache, and casein—he would often do on-the-spot drawings of proposed buildings and interior environments before any final concepts had been developed.

To this day, he is recognized in the profession of architectural delineation as one of the leading practitioners of preliminary concept sketching. He is regularly called upon by the country's leading design firms to produce series of drawings for given projects so that architects and clients can have immediate visualization of the appearance and impact of a design from views around the subject including its context in the urban landscape. With few exceptions, the sketches created by Richard Rochon contribute directly to the decision-making process of the architect and design team.

Rochon's reputation as a delineator encompasses a broad range of styles and media. His work in later years has focused primarily on pencil drawing and a clear adherence to formal graphic principles. His ability to find an essential perspective view that provides the most comprehensive orientation for depicting space while intuitively conveying a sense of scale is particularly evident in the series of drawings included throughout the book, such as Copenhagen Square, Royal Crescent, Trafalgar Square, Helsinki Market, Luxembourg Gardens, Montmartre, Parc Montsouris, Royal Palais, and O'Connelly Street.

In a client's office, Richard visualizes an architectural concept from initial discussions—the shape of the land and the space of the building. Working without preconceived ideas of what things should look like, he invests his work with qualities of exploration, spontaneity and improvisation. His ability to transform a design concept to provoke a glimpse between realism and abstraction stems from a visionary sense for pictorial drama. Often in a sketch, the pictorial design occupies him for long periods, while the main subject requires only 30 minutes.

Richard finds innumerable influences in the history of architectural illustration, commercial and fine arts, specifically illustration and painting. One of his friends, the late Robert Sutton who practiced delineation in the Midwest United States, was influential in the development of Rochon's abilities to draw expressively and quickly. Rochon admired the work of Robert Sutton that encompassed fine illustration and painting; works by Sutton, collected by museums and private collectors in the United States, served as fertile ground for experimentation and fresh visual conception. The elegance and supple manipulation of the vignette composition of Sutton was a formative experience for Rochon (I–1, I–2). Those lessons of eye movement and scanning in composition as practiced by Robert Sutton are profoundly understood by Rochon.

One can speculate on the influence of other illustrators on Richard's work. The highly decorative art of Helmut Jacoby may have had appeal, not for its exacting detail but for his use of transparency, light, and atmosphere to make a strong visual statement (I–3, I–4). During the 1950s, Robert E. Schwartz, one of the most successful practitioners in tempera paint, established a style that influenced countless young illustrators, including Rochon during his early career (I–5, I–6). In the 1970s and 1980s, Rochon pursued a period of artistic production in gouache and watercolor. Watercolor workshops with Charles Reid in Connecticut and Detroit provided a vibrant and intense experience in figure painting. Reid's lively watercolor workshops were practice of an experimental nature, and provided the opportunity to improvise with representational subject matter and often with the figure as subject. This gave Rochon great freedom to enliven and compose with a careful combination of gesture, brushwork, and disciplined representation, marking the return to a more painterly style that has continued to influence that way Richard draws today.

Many illustrators can bring forth a convincing vision of reality, impressive in technique, with a well-organized pictorial structure. However, not all illustrators or artists can create images with lasting appeal, and a haunting ability to stay in the mind. In a statement drafted by Harvey Ferrero, an architect and illustration colleague, about Rochon's work, Harvey spoke of Rochon as an illustrator:

'For as long as I have been familiar with Dick Rochon's work, he has always transcended the depiction of architecture and urban space in a merely accurate way. Often confronted with less than ideal conditions needed for a dramatic representation, his intuitive sense of composition is the solid base for his countless beautiful examples of architectural art. The problem of featuring a specific piece of architecture in its setting without underplaying its context—especially in an urban situation—is very difficult. Through the use of atmosphere, entourage, and value adjustment, Dick always succeeds in creating a picture that places the viewer in an accurate environment that is often, however, enhanced with his uncanny ability to utilize scale, texture, color, and form in the creation of these wonderful compositions.'

In the pages that follow, the art of architectural design, urban planning, and the way we view it through the use of architectural images will be demonstrated and discussed.

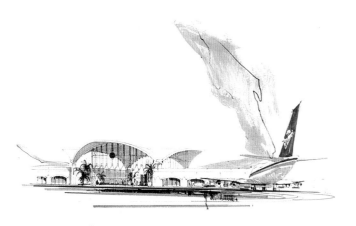

I–1 Study of exterior terminal and jet, proposal for King Fahd International Terminal, Saudi Arabia
Robert Sutton: felt pen on paper
Yamasaki and Associates

I–2 Proposed office building study sketch
Richard Rochon: colored pencil

The focus of this book is not only urban design, but also the images that both inspire urban architecture and reflect the outcome of building. Moreover, a special emphasis is placed on both elegant examples of historic urban design and architecture as well as contemporary urban architecture and design. It is the purpose of this book to underscore the interdependence of the discipline of architectural illustration and the art of architecture and urban design. Both of these disciplines interact and inform each other and in doing so contribute to the flourishing of great vision in design.

Examples both historic and contemporary, of work from some of the world's most outstanding architects and urban planners, are rendered by Richard Rochon largely in colored pencil to demonstrate elements of design and visual communications— mass, volume and space, gesture, movement, content and intent, as well as shade and shadow, color, and atmosphere. Finally, examples of building-directed idea representation as design investigation are emphasized. The discussion of groups of drawings is made to explore the question of how these types of drawings interact, support, define, and contribute to the eventual design. Furthermore, discussion is focused on what these images have to say of our humanity and behavior as reflections of the built environment.

It is hoped that the reader will discover in the words and images represented here that the architect seeking to design a more useful and more beautiful environment is better served by the art of visual representation. The grace of an inspired hand in service of the designer's vision demonstrates the larger context of a creative process whose trajectory is a better environment and whose real purpose is a more beautiful world.

The corpus of Richard Rochon's work included here is a portfolio of the creative arc of his oeuvre. These 175 drawings, representative of historic urban spaces and buildings throughout the world, built and unbuilt, provide a full source of creative and technical inspiration for artists, architects, designers and planners of the urban landscape.

His profound technical mastery, his precise draftsmanship, and his romanticism and humanity captured within theatrical illustrative designs form a meditation on the quality of 20th-century urban architecture.

These essentially 'modern impressions' are the result of a prolific creative intelligence grasping for the expressive vitality of an architecture and its image. The process of illustration is often, by its very nature, the motivating force for an illustrator rather than its physical result—the building. Yet, in the work of Richard Rochon, the illustrative process is inextricably linked to the kernel of the architect's vision and the manifestation of this physical reality and its impact in the urban landscape.

I–3 Ford Foundation Headquarters, New York City
Helmut Jacoby: ink and airbrush
Courtesy of Helmut Jacoby and the Ford Foundation

I–4 Tampa Courthouse, Tampa, Florida
Richard Rochon: colored pencil
Hellmuth, Obata + Kassabaum (HOK), Inc. (Tampa)

This book showcases a unique collection of full color drawings created with superb artistry and instrumentation. The illustrator's choice of medium is largely colored pencil, however, sometimes combined with watercolor wash beneath pencil and sometimes combined with tonal qualities from initial sketch foundations in graphite. Renderings of both historic and contemporary architecture will provide a panoramic view of not only the qualities of urban architecture and public space, but also of the delight of visualization—of bringing to life, light, and public forum—the evolutionary and engaging designs of public spaces.

Rochon's carefully crafted and readable architectural drawings are lucid manifestations of the architect's process depicting the materials of buildings and the landscape in the full spectrum of color, light, form and space. Buildings inspire drawings and in so doing lead to an interdependence of illustration, architecture, and the built environment. In the works carefully chosen for this presentation, the inspiration of architecture in urban settings finds its origins in the architect's schemes—the building and environmental elements, materials, scale, and arrangement of all these ideas in a final design solution. The ideal world of the architect's imagination meets the illustrator's fertile and conceptual reservoir of images, adding, subtracting, and informing the act of architectural design.

What better relationship can occur other than the symbiosis of two related and yet distinguishable disciplines in harmonic convergence with one another? The confluence of the most humanistic art of architecture with the exacting perception of the architectural artist flows together to form a unison of planning and achievement. From the freehand sketch as a record of the design process throughout the length of the project revealing the inner workings of the architect's mind, the architectural illustrator as a trusted guide provides marvelous examples of the true invention of the architecture as an altogether superior artistic achievement. The renderings of Richard Rochon present a powerful example of urban visions and are a provocative instrument that conveys the essence of the urban landscape—to dream of ideas about cityscape or architecture and its influence.

I–5 88 Pine Street, New York City
Robert E Schwartz: tempera
Pei Cobb Freed & Partners

I–6 Aloha Tower, Honolulu, Hawaii
Richard Rochon: tempera
Arquitectonica

ACKNOWLEDGEMENTS

This project would not have happened without the support of many people. I am deeply grateful to David Childs for his insightful foreword that reflects a deep appreciation for the artistry of Richard Rochon. David Childs' experience reaches across a lifetime of excellence in architecture and professional practice and embraces a unique symbiosis of architecture and illustration. I am equally indebted to Elizabeth Plater-Zyberk for her remarks and seminal works that embrace the cultural imperatives of urban renewal with innovative and groundbreaking planning for the rebirth of urban spaces throughout the world.

I am indebted to my friend and colleague, Richard Rochon, whose work and vision over several decades has inspired this author. The corpus of his portfolio reaches an ever-higher plateau of aesthetic accomplishment with each and every new body of work. The artistry produced especially for this book is as much about a passion for drawing as it regards a lifetime commitment to the renewal of our city centers and neighborhoods. His consummate artistry, demonstrated throughout this book in considerable ways and means, reflects an unsurpassed passion to promote urban projects that positively impact the way we live, interact, participate, and enjoy the built environment.

This book would not have been possible if it were not for the kind advice of Joseph Demkin of the American Institute of Architects, and Paul Latham and Alessina Brooks of The Images Publishing Group, Melbourne, Australia. They believed that Richard's work and the concept for a book of urban illustrations were interwoven and fused together over a lifetime of artistic accomplishment with expert visualization and the ambition for a realization of great urban places.

Numerous others were involved in bringing the material to life. Special thanks go to the staff of Rochon Associates, including Jerry Rochon and Annette Boyer, assisted by Christine Gonzalez, for working tirelessly and responding to requests for research material and information; and to Dennis DiCello for his contribution of site photographs. A special thanks to Joanne Rochon, graphic designer and artist, for her numerous on-site photographs—they were inspiring in viewpoint and composition. Our love to Carol Kaffenberger, who imagined a place where historic urban design is celebrated for its lasting charm and elegance, and for its influence on the future. We wish to especially thank Nadyne Linton for the figure captions that accompany the illustrations in the book—her poetic articulation of the life of urban space is a special gift to the book.

NORTH AMERICAN URBANISM

The Italian word *modelli* is sometimes used to suggest drawings as preliminary studies for a rendering. Because renderings are intended to impress a prospective client, they are often more finished than the sketches made by the artist for his/her own use during the creation of the work. Helping the client to see what a proposed design will look like, and enabling the designer to discuss alternatives, are the objectives of more refined illustrations.

Illustrations made well before the design is built are usually created in an effort to win a design commission or contract. The clarity of their form and description stems from the illustrator's skill in visualizing what the intended design concept will look like, often along with its landscaping, building material, and/or interior design scheme. These works can be appreciated for their aesthetic qualities alone, without thought to the original reason for their existence, which is nevertheless an important factor contributing to their appearance. Rochon's ability to generate a strong sense of graphic space in drawings of urban environments is due to his refined ability to maintain strong surface control. Curiously, it is through the realization of three-dimensional form and color illusion that the evolution of original graphic space is possible.

Many of these illustrations forecast the constantly evolving patterns and styles of urban architecture and planning, well ahead of the physical existence of the construction of a building and/or environment. The relationship between architecture and public space in North American cities is evolving into new directions of diversity, pedestrian scale, spatial organization, and new formations of neighborhoods. These drawings capture the changing patterns, spatial hierarchy and connectedness of new urban spaces. Whether of single-family neighborhoods, the commercial sector, high-rise projects, or high- and low-density urban renewal, they can easily be appreciated for their visionary appeal as explorations of the future.

The new direction in planning today acknowledges that the city, suburbs and the natural environment should be treated as a whole—socially, economically and ecologically.

A new vision for urban design proposes that the metropolis should be designed with the same attitude as we design a neighborhood. Boundaries and edges are defined, with enhanced pedestrian circulation systems through sidewalks and regional transit systems, purposeful formation of public spaces, and a balance between affordable housing and employment opportunities—all at a range of densities and scales and in all regions of the country.

The rebirth of pedestrian walkways and urban shopping areas exemplified in Old Montreal (Figure 1–1), King Street (Figure 1–4), and Vancouver Waterfront (Figure 1–5) is captured in an atmosphere of bright illumination that brings a unified tonal range with bursts of color and light/dark contrasts of form. The eye dances across points of interest and is directed toward strong areas of illumination. In the United States Embassy (Figures 1–2, 1–3), Douglas Park (Figures 1–7, 1–8), Old South Meeting House (Figure 1–9), and Quincy Market (Figure 1–10), a unified scheme of lighting and color palette underscores the urban theme of busy pedestrian walkways and commercial centers, while also serving as a focal point and a foil for contrasts in coloration. Buckingham Fountain (Figure 1–13), Grant Park Waterfront (Figure 1–15), and Outdoor Café (Figure 1–16) communicate a bright, sunlit summer afternoon in a restful urban oasis. From parks to courtyards, the qualities of dappled sunlight and a bright sunny palette add charm and nuance to the clothing, grass, water, and related entourage of the urban oasis.

The University of Chicago Graduate School of Business (Figure 1–17), North Coast Harbor (Figure 1–18), and Dallas Main Center II (Figure 1–19) gain drama from the pictorial design of a focal point of illumination and the application of carefully controlled nuances of hue and value. Each of these urban environments provides images of architecture where the color value and tonal range are highly controlled and carefully orchestrated. The play of color scales in various ranges from light to dark and bright to dull allows the architectural subject to subtly emerge from the pictorial space to engage the viewer.

If the size and shape of the drawing surface or support is of little or no importance in the layout, design, and construction of an illustration, the picture is usually called an *open* composition. A small illustration executed in the middle of a relatively large drawing sheet is little influenced by the edges of the paper and therefore appears to float on the sheet, unaffected by the empty surround. When borders limit the size and shape of an illustration, it is usually referred to as a *closed* picture. The artist can create the borders, or the limit can be imposed by the edges of the drawing surface, in technical terms a *bleed*. The many variations between open and closed pictorial design hold creative possibilities for compositions of beautiful illustrative subject matter. Focusing the imagination on the possibilities of the pictorial space on the page can lead to myriad new constructions of space-form composition.

The illustrations of projects in Detroit, Michigan that follow are created as *closed* compositions to provide a picture postcard atmosphere for the content. The Detroit Urban Revitalization Proposal I, II, and III (Figures 1–20 to 1–22) are all proposals seeking support from city and federal government as well as the private sector. The purpose of these renderings is to portray the urban revitalization and urban landscape in a positive and pleasing summer setting with people posed in natural daily activity. The limits of the illustrations are softened and enhanced with plant materials, trees, people sitting on chairs at tables, and of course the typical summertime blue sky.

Prominent urban development proposals of great popularity in Detroit are illustrated in the context of their most natural setting as evening entertainment venues. The Motown Museum Expansion (Figure 1–23) and Theater District (Figure 1–26) demonstrate the special qualities of dramatic natural and artificial evening illumination. Stroh Properties' River Place development project along the Detroit River (Figures 1–24, 1–25), exemplifies the refurbishment of a once-industrial manufacturing zone of brick-exterior buildings into a mixed-use residential condominium and commercial park-like sector.

The entertainment and cultural spirit is alive and well throughout North America with exciting new museums, parks, and amusements opening each year. The illustrations of the Newark Arena Expansion project demonstrate a design where the activity of people—along with an emphasis on appropriate signage, kiosks, plant materials, and architectural features—makes for a vital and engaging spatial composition (Figures 1–30, 1–31). In the Japanese American National Museum (Figure 1–29) and Pacific Trade Center (Figure 1–28), aerial views depict building plans for pedestrian walkways, parking, building entrance and adjacent neighborhoods.

The role of illustrations for redevelopment is to fashion drawings into broad views of architectural content, including the representation of the context of other buildings and adjacent neighborhoods. The density of urban life in New York is an especially challenging problem for architects and urban planners, and also for illustrators. How does the artist depict the main subject without including numerous other buildings adjacent to it? A portfolio of illustrations from the work of David M. Childs at Skidmore, Owings & Merrill, New York (Figures 1–32 to 1–45) is included to demonstrate the diversity of urban architectural design challenges from residential, entertainment, and office complexes, including mixed-use small and large urban developments. Each of these drawings was created with the purpose of framing the main subject. The technique of softening detail in adjacent buildings and neighborhoods acts as a vignette, providing contrast and distinguishing the main building form(s) from all of the others. The technique is achromatic, yet the atmosphere achieved originates in the carefully controlled stipple technique of the illustrator as a nod to Helmut Jacoby and the international style of architecture and illustration of the 1950s.

Within the bustle of commerce and development in New York, one can still find those places that afford a respite from the cacophony of noise and traffic that characterize it as a mecca for international trade and business (Figures 1–46, 1–47). The island of Manhattan is dotted with more than 90 parks of various sizes, beginning, of course, with Central Park at the core (Figures 1–48, 1–49). There are, however, numerous smaller parks, plazas, and urban spaces that afford pedestrians distraction and an opportunity for relaxation. Hudson Park Pond (Figure 1–50), Washington Market Park (Figure 1–55), Union Square Park (Figure 1–57), and Hudson Park Walkway (Figure 1–58) are excellent examples of those spaces in between buildings and plazas that pedestrians find as an oasis within the city. They are rendered with full palette and in full daylight with an impressionistic atmosphere of drawing stroke layered upon stroke. The result is a rich tapestry of mark-making that captures the essence of form through color and pattern, and the bucolic nature of open space within the city.

Scandinavia House in New York illustrates the natural appearance of the streetscape with adjacent buildings and attracts the viewer's attention to a reflective glass entryway (Figure 1–56). The artistry of the illustration demonstrates how a rendering of a reflective glass façade can be distinguished from its environment through visual cues such as the flags of the Scandinavian countries.

Fifteenth Street Tower in Philadelphia offers a dramatically different vantage point as an illustration of a high-density urban environment (Figure 1–59). The aerial point of view is used to distinguish the building form and its location within the city and provides a level of contrast and definition to the building profile against the city skyline.

Main Street Plaza in Salt Lake City, Utah is an eerie drawing in golden light with strong symmetrical orientation to the main subject, Temple Square Development (Figures 1–62, 1–63). The sky reflected in the pool helps frame and soften the silhouette of the temple and focus attention on its form and its reflection at the center of the composition.

The San Antonio River Walk rises and falls across pedestrian bridges and tree-canopied pathways beside outdoor cafés, public plazas, benches, and a densely landscaped urban pathway along the riverside (Figure 1–64). As one of the most popular and successful urban design projects in Texas, this very successful public attraction draws visitors from around the country and abroad to delight in the journey by foot, bicycle, or boat as the river promenade meanders gently through the city of San Antonio.

Washington D.C. exemplifies the grand manner of city planning based on schemes designed by Major Pierre L'Enfant and commissioned by President George Washington in 1791. L'Enfant planned the capital in the characteristic style of the Baroque esthetic with a grid and overlaid avenues directed principally as spokes, and grand tree-lined boulevards to connect and thereby shorten the real distance from place to place. Reciprocity of sight is also provided, making the expanse of boulevards seemingly connect a grand spacious urban ensemble pinned on four points of distribution throughout the city.

Federal buildings are aligned to the master plan based on the L'Enfant model of vistas and therefore can be appreciated as integral to the main sight lines of the original city plan. The Federal Triangle and Pershing Park illustrations reflect the important elements of wide boulevards, tree-lined streets and the campus-like quality of the interior courts and walkways (Figures 1–68 to 1–70).

Worcester Center demonstrates an aerial view of the city of Worcester, Massachusetts and an overview of the city plan with radial and grid formations integrated into a cohesive whole (Figure 1–72). This multi-use urban mall incorporates business, retail, and residential spaces. It is a microcosm of the urban experience—a symbol of urbanity—that is an environment for living that is ultimately a product of human imagination and endeavor.

The works in this section demonstrate that the symbol or metaphor for an urban environment is bound up in the over-arching reason for the illustration, originating in the dream of the architect and planner, and in the imagination of the artist. The dream of fulfilling the promise of the architecture through the creation of the illustration is to imbue the subject with a force greater than the depiction of an environment. Just as the 20th-century impressionists immersed their subject matter in a sea of color and light, an atmospheric effect communicates not only the reality of space but the feeling of forces in nature that take precedence over a portrayal of factual events.

1–1 Old Montreal, Montreal, Canada
A dense pocket of provincial and classic ornamentation on building façades coalesces into a busy commercial district of shops and eateries

1–2 United States Embassy, Ottawa, Canada
United States Embassy sited with Canadian Parliament
buildings in background
Skidmore, Owings & Merrill (Washington, D.C.)

1–3 United States Embassy, Ottawa, Canada
Skidmore, Owings & Merrill (Washington, D.C.)

1–5 Vancouver Waterfront, Vancouver, British Columbia
One could be walking onto a stage set with large contemporary buildings forming a panoramic urban backdrop to the view of the water

Opposite: 1–4 King Street, Toronto, Canada
Serene three-story buildings—industrial, pragmatic, and rediscovered, are preserved
for adaptation in a new century to commercial and residential use

1–6 Naval Systems Command Center, Arlington, Virginia
Curvilinear vertical planes in the atrium with transparent walkways form a dramatic interior environment
Skidmore, Owings & Merrill (New York)

28

1–7 Douglas Park, Boston, Massachusetts
This contemporary mixed-use retail and residential
development melds with its historic context through the
appropriate use of color, materials, and scale
ADD Inc.

1–8 Douglas Park, Boston, Massachusetts
Brick façades and sidewalk edges are features that add
warmth and texture to new urban townhouses
ADD Inc.

1–10 Quincy Market, Boston, Massachusetts
This is a place where business people and strollers feel comfortable rubbing shoulders—the open quality
of the market provides an invitation to explore and commune with friends and new acquaintances

Opposite: 1–9 Old South Meeting House, Boston, Massachusetts
As if one were a time-traveler to a city of historic American architecture distinct in color, texture
and scale, and well-suited when viewed against the high-rise modern towers in the distance

1–11 Charleston Place, Charleston, South Carolina
The French Provincial style of these commercial buildings with their light palette of colors and materials similar to the surroundings, promotes a sense of continuity with the surrounding community and an ease of living and shopping with everything at one's fingertips
Taubman Associates

1–12 Charleston Place, Charleston, South Carolina
Taubman Associates

1–13 Buckingham Fountain, Grant Park, Chicago, Illinois
'This space is extremely large and enjoys a great deal of landscaping. It is used by a variety of public groups from band concerts to soccer games.' — Leslie H. Kenyon, Kenyon & Associates, Architects

1–14 Blue Cross Blue Shield, Chicago, Illinois
Phase Two Blue Cross Blue Shield office tower in Grant Park
Lohan Associates

Opposite: 1–15 Grant Park Waterfront, Chicago, Illinois
'What remarkable self-control on the part of the city fathers to offer the lakefront as a series of parks and places to the citizens of Chicago. While other cities filled their precious waterfronts with early 20th-century industry, Chicago set in place the framework for this remarkable urban shore.' — William Hartman, Gensler Architects

1–16 Outdoor Café, The Museum of the Art Institute of Chicago, Chicago, Illinois
It is easy to transport oneself to an Italian Piazza when in fact this lovely eatery is in the heart of the Art Institute of Chicago

1–17 University of Chicago Graduate School of Business, Chicago, Illinois
Not at all confining, the numerous, large windows at street level and reflecting pool contribute to the sense of transparency, reflection, and spaciousness
Skidmore, Owings & Merrill (Chicago)

1–18 Northcoast Harbor, Cleveland, Ohio

A proposed development surrounding I. M. Pei's 'Rock & Roll Hall of Fame', the harbor's fingers reach out to invite and entice visitors to explore and delight in the public venues at the lakefront
GSI Architects, Inc.

1–20 Urban Revitalization Proposal I, Detroit, Michigan
The revitalized Detroit waterfront is an invitation to families to stroll along the river on a weekend afternoon, in the shadow of the impressive Renaissance Office Complex
Smith Group

1–21 Urban Revitalization Proposal II, Detroit, Michigan
The contemporary appearance of the public transportation is complemented by the nostalgic appearance of the storefronts and their close proximity to the pedestrian walkways on Woodward Avenue
Smith Group

1–22 Urban Revitalization Proposal III, Detroit, Michigan
New designs for urban development of streets feature outdoor cafés, ample sidewalks, new street lighting, and banners
Smith Group

Opposite: 1–19 Dallas Main Center II, Dallas, Texas
A profound statement of transparency with dramatic evening illumination
Skidmore, Owings & Merrill (Chicago)

North American Urbanism **39**

1–23 Motown Museum Expansion, Detroit, Michigan
The proposed Motown Museum expansion built around the original Motown houses is a tribute to the 'Motown' sound on a grand scale, full of light and life
Paul Matelic Architects

1–24 Stroh River Place, Masterplan and Renovation, Detroit, Michigan
This office and retail conversion of the former Parke-Davis Pharmaceuticals building on Detroit's waterfront is inconspicuous and expansive, two qualities that provide an encompassing attraction to the public
Polshek and Partners

1–25 Stroh River Place, Masterplan and Renovation, Detroit, Michigan
Plaza view
Polshek and Partners

1–26 Theater District, Detroit, Michigan
The theater district on Woodward Avenue in Detroit is a prime example of the rebirth of Detroit's urban center

44

Opposite: 1–27 Hines Downriver Tower, Houston, Texas
A structure of curves and corners complements the adjacent buildings
Hellmuth, Obata + Kassabaum (HOK), Inc. (Houston)

1–28 Pacific Trade Center, Los Angeles, California
A topiary garden draws attention to the summit
Hellmuth, Obata + Kassabaum (HOK), Inc. (Los Angeles)

**1–29 Japanese American National Museum,
Los Angeles, California**
The curvilinear façade presents a 'soft' corner building
entrance with open plaza
Hellmuth, Obata + Kassabaum (HOK), Inc. (Los Angeles)

1–30 Newark Arena Expansion, Newark, New Jersey
Skidmore, Owings & Merrill (New York)

1–31 Newark Arena Expansion, Newark, New Jersey
Inherently playful color, architectural forms, and super graphics help to define the Newark Arena Expansion
Skidmore, Owings & Merrill (New York)

1–33 Columbus Circle, 2000, New York
Study drawing
Skidmore, Owings & Merrill (New York)

Opposite: 1–32 Columbus Circle, 1993, New York
Columbus Center is the vertical integration of multiple urban uses including parking, retail, movie theaters, offices, and residences. The challenge of bringing disparate adjoining neighborhoods together with a new commercial and residential hub is an important dimension of the planning for this project.
Skidmore, Owings & Merrill (New York)

1–34 Madison Square Garden Site Development, New York
In collaboration with Frank Gehry, this proposal would add two
new office towers to the site of Manhattan's Pennsylvania Station
Skidmore, Owings & Merrill (New York)

1–35 Madison Square Garden Site Development, New York
Interior view of the Great Hall
Skidmore, Owings & Merrill (New York)

1–36 450 Lexington Avenue, New York
Aerial perspective
Skidmore, Owings & Merrill (New York)

1–37 Tribeca Pedestrian Bridge, New York
This pedestrian bridge in Battery Park rises like the
sun above the street
Skidmore, Owings & Merrill (New York)

1–38 Tribeca Pedestrian Bridge, New York
The Tribeca Bridge spans West Street as it enters Lower Manhattan, linking students from across the city
with the front door of Stuyvesant High School and linking the residents of adjoining neighborhoods with
a new waterfront park
Skidmore, Owings & Merrill (New York)

Opposite: 1–39 One Broadway Place, New York
Changes to city zoning in the Times Square District
allowed for a massive introduction of new office space
in a manner that would not imperil the vibrant retail
and entertainment uses
Skidmore, Owings & Merrill (New York)

1–40 320 Park Avenue, 1993, New York
Perspective
Skidmore, Owings & Merrill (New York)

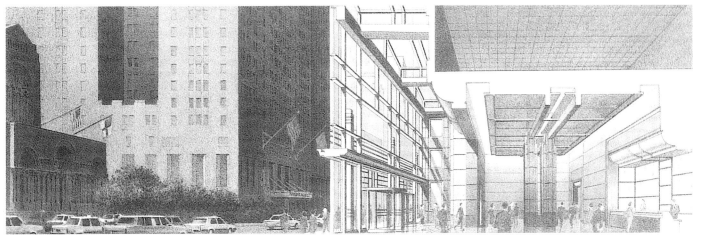

1–41 320 Park Avenue, 1993, New York
A sectional perspective of the lobby and Park Avenue looking south
Skidmore, Owings & Merrill (New York)

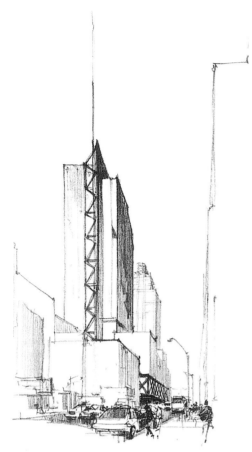

1–43 Port Authority Bus Terminal, New York
Sketch study
Skidmore, Owings & Merrill (New York)

1–42 320 Park Avenue, 1990, New York
Although several buildings along the posh Park Avenue corridor have reached the end
of their economic life, many are architectural landmarks that will eventually be renewed. This
development project will restore function and performance, and will reshape a 1960s building
into a vibrant part of the 21st-century workplace.
Skidmore, Owings & Merrill (New York)

1–44 Memorial Sloan Kettering, New York
Study drawing
Skidmore, Owings & Merrill (New York)

Opposite: 1–45 Riverside South, New York
Riverside South clings to the banks of the Hudson River and reclaims industrial land once
inaccessible and unusable. This newly proposed project introduces residential units, a center
for television and movie production, street-front shopping, and an expansive riverfront park.
Skidmore, Owings & Merrill (New York)

1–46 Bike Path at Broadway, New York
Urban planners soften the lanes of traffic with planters and flowers,
a human-scale invitation to travel the bicycle lanes on the way home

Opposite top: 1–47 Bus Stop at Central Park, New York
The busy pedestrian and street traffic does not diminish the ability
of a Central Park bus stop to soften the edges of the city

Opposite bottom: 1–48 Central Park Book Fair, New York
Book fairs near Central Park are a welcome venue for public enjoyment

1–49 Central Park, New York
'This grand park feels natural and completely urban at the same time' — Cesar Pelli, Cesar Pelli & Associates Architects

Opposite: 1–50 Hudson Park Pond, New York
Pedestrians are grateful to find nature in the city, whether on a work or play day

1–51 NYU Law School at Washington Square Park, New York
Aerial view
Kohn Pedersen Fox

1–52 NYU Law School, New York
The curvilinear peak of the top of the building brings the eye down through a terrace of cascading setbacks that soften the appearance of the mass of the building
Kohn Pedersen Fox

1–53 NYU Law School, New York
Kohn Pedersen Fox

1–54 NYU Law School, New York
Washington Square Park with the Law School in the distance
Kohn Pedersen Fox

1–55 Washington Market Park, New York
A beautiful canopy of trees imparts an inviting feeling of enclosure and security, essential to a children's play area

1–56 Scandinavia House, New York
A proposed renovation of a townhouse into an art gallery and community center
Albert Kahn Associates

1–57 Union Square Park, New York
A moment of serenity is magnified when sitting in the presence of a garden park in Manhattan

1–58 Walkway, Hudson Park, New York
This inviting pathway is a reflective environment for preparing oneself mentally for the tasks ahead (especially on a Monday)

1–60 Rittenhouse Square Park, Philadelphia, Pennsylvania
A city center park close to high-rise office towers is designed for human delight with curvilinear pathways, numerous places to rest and converse, and brick pavers, which add texture to the streetscape

Opposite: 1–59 Fifteenth Street Tower, Philadelphia, Pennsylvania
The business tower strikes a distinctive profile as it rises amidst the dense Philadelphia skyline
Rossetti Associates

1–61 Museum of Railroad Technology, Sacramento, California

It is a comfortable train ride into rail history when walking through the Museum of Railroad Technology in Sacramento. The gentle, snaking movement of this structure is enhanced by its proximity to the water.

Cambridge Seven Associates

1–62 Gateway Center, Salt Lake City, Utah

Large office tower anchors the campus for the Temple Square Development

MHTN Architects

1–63 Main Street Plaza Reflecting Pool, Salt Lake City, Utah
The Temple Square Development at Main Street Plaza with reflecting pond is an oasis for personal reflection in the city
MHTN Architects

1–64 Riverwalk, San Antonio, Texas
The plan of enclosing a waterway with rising, falling and bending pathways makes the Riverwalk a delightful adventure of dreamy reflection. Nuances of light and color, variations in scale and perspective, and places to relax all contribute to a sense of losing oneself in passageways that meander through time and space.

Opposite: 1–65 Yerba Buena Office Towers, San Francisco, California
The large glass windows at street level help to attract visitors to the lobby space
Skidmore, Owings & Merrill (New York)

1–66 Van Ness Residential, San Francisco, California
The clever architectural design of the Van Ness Residential building in San Francisco affords the lucky tenants extraordinary views, regardless of their interior location
Skidmore, Owings & Merrill (San Francisco)

1–67 Stanford University, Stanford, California
Aerial view
Pei Cobb Freed & Partners

1–70 Federal Triangle, Washington D.C.
Completed addition to Federal Triangle
Pei Cobb Freed & Partners

Opposite top: 1–68 Federal Triangle, Washington D.C.
The surrounding buildings with landscape features are oriented to define a courtyard space,
add scale to the street and sidewalks, and convey a feeling of the scale of an urban campus
Hellmuth, Obata + Kassabaum (HOK), Inc. (Washington)

Opposite bottom: 1–69 Federal Triangle, Washington D.C.
Hellmuth, Obata + Kassabaum (HOK), Inc. (Washington)

1–71 Pershing Square at Pennsylvania Avenue, Washington D.C.
When walking through the park, the simplicity of an elegant and contemplative environment presents the atmosphere of calm necessary to prepare oneself for the tasks ahead

1–72 Worcester Center, Worcester, Massachusetts

An aerial of new civic mixed use office, retail and residential development complex

Arrowstreet Associates

The illustrator's power of visualization springs from an intense study of the built environment and also from a keen perception and sensitive understanding of the architecture. The extension of the present into a reality yet unknown is based in part on the precise and objective requirements of an illustration, and also a requisite fluency in portraying the physical attributes of architecture in any cultural context, anywhere throughout the world. What makes most major cities in the world interesting to draw are the people who shape the culture and environment, and in turn, lend a unique character to the qualities of life and design.

Predicting the appearance of future environments is the specific responsibility of the architectural illustrator. In the 1980s, the concept of *de-urbanization* sprang forth from controversy about the 'death of cities' and from what had been called *neo-ruralization*—the growth of suburban towns and the urban fringe. Illustrators confronted the new pictorial reality of portraying a 'work-in-progress'—suburban development throughout the world. Urban flight to the suburbs offered contextual demands for illustrators of how to deal with new towns and high-rise projects in a rural context. This trend of suburban development, however, is confronted by the latest census returns from the 1980s and 1990s. The city, in fact, and even the large city, is far from disappearing. From the least developed to the most advanced economies, indications site that cities are not in decline but are in a new and dynamic state of transformation.

The processes of industrialization and rapid urbanization in the economies of the southern hemisphere—Sub-Saharan Africa, India, Central and South America—are resulting in shifts that can be seen through the decline of rural areas. In addition, they are clearly linked and exacerbated through patterns of migration and the relocation of populations to cities. Greater densities of population act upon and reshape cities and suburbs of the southern hemisphere, resulting in a compounding of spatial qualities and attributes of urban circulation. These aspects of urban density, beginning with migration, relocation, dislocation, and destabilization, have become main features of urban experience. In turn, this has precipitated new theories and cartographies of space, forms, and iconographies of living and dwelling, strategies of urban development, infrastructure, architecture, and the associated physical reality of urban planning experienced in architectural illustration.

2–1 Plaza San Martin, Buenos Aires, Argentina
'It is in reality a tiny park, beautifully planted, and a place where one can spend hours with a book
or a friend in the heart of the city' — Cesar Pelli, Cesar Pelli & Associates Architects

Many signs tell us that the phenomenon of urban migration is affecting contemporary cities. On the one hand, we can observe the interruption and even the inversion of centuries-old urbanization processes; on the other, there is a growing renewed interest in urban life where attractive images of new technologies mix with the disquieting promises of a new urban middle age, à la 'Gotham city.' More and more people are trying to survive in cities with less and less. In spite of this, people act on the city, and give shape to the city, as the city acts on them. The illustrator fuses the new urbanity and density with architecture and entourage to arrive at a synthesis of realities—a considered transformation faithful to both the architecture and the forces shaping the environmental context.

Urbanity in South American cities originates with centuries-old traditions and the romance of public parks, gardens, plazas and places for recreation, sports and entertainment. Plaza San Martin, in Buenos Aires, Argentina is a magnificent example of a pristine promenade through gardens and pathways of the most splendid floral specimens and landscaping (Figure 2–1). Modernist visions of urban space are still a very prominent element in the minds of urban architects, planners and policy makers. Puerto Madero, Buenos Aires, Argentina, proposes a resort entertainment complex. Its main purpose is to draw tourists from an ever-widening international travel market, similar to Puerto Vallarta, Baja Peninsula, Acapulco, and even Liverpool Docks, where the redevelopment of dilapidated docks in an urban setting was completely revitalized (Figures 2–2 to 2–4). Club Atletico, in Curitiba, Brazil provides recreation and athletic facilities of high visual profile with appealing super graphics, playful architecture and amenities of park-like setting and a major stadium/amphitheater for sporting competitions and entertainment (Figures 2–5, 2–6).

The architectural history of South American cities such as Santiago, Chile and Cartagena, Columbia reflects historic monuments and architecture in context with the intimate scale of buildings in their natural settings (Figures 2–8 to 2–10). Latin American cities have undergone a number of significant changes in the last decade. The revitalization and beautification of historic centers, monuments, city parks, and especially streets and major plazas, are points of national pride and leading attributes in the attraction of innovative new urban renewal, international investment, and infrastructure revitalization. Plaza de la Catedral, Havana, Cuba stands as one of the most revered public plazas in the world with centuries of architectural heritage—a poetic space of wondrous human

scale, ornamentation and antiquity (Figure 2–11). Inspired by indigenous Incan architecture, The United States Embassy in Lima, Peru is a clear example of a playful and post-modern government building design in a checkerboard motif that encompasses the plaza, building façade and adjacent urban spaces (Figure 2–15).

Community improvement districts in major African cities are contributing to urban renewal by providing enclaves of business partnerships that have privatized all of the attributes that make a city hum—cafés, magazine stands, pharmacies, hairdressers, and stationers under one roof. These mega-business oases are anchored by the largest of Africa's banks and lending institutions and have formed partnerships for urban development similar to their counterparts in suburbia throughout the world (Figure 2–13). The nature of western mindsets and how they organize space and politics as urban and rural, is being challenged as the reprioritization and sovereignty of nation-states present determinants for alternate forms of globalization and urban development.

Although there is a growing 'world-class city' mantra directed at investors in many of the largest urban centers of the southern hemisphere, it is often not connected to everyday life and does not inspire a collective identity. In Johannesburg for example, the words, the sentiment, the images with which most people identify, and to which they aspire are the homogeneous shopping malls or 'Tuscon' villas that proliferate in the northern suburbs or in the culturally rich townships. The Sandton phenomenon to the north of Johannesburg signifies the development of an 'edge city'. However, its existence is in part a response to conditions that cannot be equated to a central suburb, and also draws significance from a broader regional, inter-urban, context. In Capetown, new office high-rises are under construction as urban centers undergo infrastructure improvements and an infusion of industrial and commercial development (Figures 2–16, 2–17). The illustration of the downtown district in Harare, Zimbabwe best reflects the state of urbanity in developing nations in the southern hemisphere—the wonder of contrasts—where the west meets local culture, finding itself in a state of expansion of global dimensions (Figure 2–18).

2–2 Parcel 17, Puerto Madero, Buenos Aires, Argentina
An encompassing, self-contained recreational and entertainment environment
Hellmuth, Obata + Kassabaum, Inc. (St. Louis)

Opposite top: 2–3 Puerto Madero, Buenos Aires, Argentina
Puerto Madero, the former port of Buenos Aires, is a spectacular and booming area
now converted into a beautiful 3-mile-long commercial district with more than 60
different restaurants, resort hotels, and many new important international offices
Hellmuth, Obata + Kassabaum, Inc. (St. Louis)

Opposite bottom: 2–4 Puerto Madero, Buenos Aires, Argentina
Hellmuth, Obata + Kassabaum, Inc. (St. Louis)

2–5 Club Atletico, Curitiba, Brazil
Sports Stadium complex with brilliantly colored
architectural details, super graphics, and a dramatic
massing of architectural forms, creates an atmosphere
of excitement, and is a great attraction
GSI Architects

2–6 Club Atletico, Curitiba, Brazil
Aerial view
GSI Architects

2–7 Municipal Theater, Rio de Janeiro, Brazil
Modeled after the Paris Opera and located in the city core, a spacious plaza characterizes the theater which
opened in 1909, showcasing the greatest musicians, singers, and dancers from around the world

2–8 Piazza de Armas, Santiago, Chile
This is the central point of the city from which all distances are measured; it is surrounded by Museo Historico Nacional and La Catedral. The clever placement of the vegetation and sculpture naturally direct visitors to the plaza toward the monument, which is its main focus.

2–9 Ascensor Mojitas, Valparaiso, Chile
'This 19th-century construction that pierces through the city, creates an intertwining system of terraces, stairs, pathways and residences. This singular integration of architecture, abrupt landscape, views, social practices and Valparaiso's famed "ascensores" (lifts), constructs a density of experiences that make the city a cinematic event' — Patricio del Real, Clemson University

2–10 Walled City, Cartagena, Columbia
Founded in 1533, this small city on Columbia's Caribbean coast is a well-preserved example of Spanish colonial architecture. It was fortified with walls in 1640–1657 by African slaves, who were literally worked to death. As many as 40,000 slaves may have died, their bodies unceremoniously thrown into the sea.

2–11 Plaza de la Catedral, Havana, Cuba

'This plaza is perhaps one of the most sophisticated urban Baroque spaces in the world. The obliqueness of its approach, the subtle asymmetry of its composition, and the invading buildings through archways form an ambiguous space, create an urban room of great intimacy and surprise' — Patricio del Real, Clemson University

2–12 Roundabout, Bangalore, India
Bangalore, the capital of Karnataka State and India's fifth-largest city, is also called the Garden City and boasts a great many parks, flowering tree-lined streets and roundabouts

2–13 Central City Square, Nairobi, Kenya
The Square is surrounded by the city hall, Kenya's parliament, the Kenyatta Conference Center, the courts and the mausoleum of Jomo Kenyatta, Kenya's founding father. The statue is of Jomo Kenyatta, the 'light of Kenya'.

2–14 Plaza de San Martin, Lima, Peru
A historic district celebrating the memory of Jose de San Martin, liberator and protector of Peru

Southern Hemisphere Transformations **93**

2–15 US Embassy, Lima, Peru
The post-modern design establishes
a strong playful patterning on the
building façade and plaza floor that
is complemented by the openness of
its surroundings and nature-filled
environment
Arquitectonica

2–16 Cape Town with Table Mountain, Cape Town, South Africa
City parks like this are uncommon in urban centers in Africa. A new high-rise office tower is complemented by Table Mountain and city park.

2–17 Cape Town City Hall, Cape Town, South Africa
The most impressive feature of Cape Town City Hall is the opulently decorated marble façade which combines Italian renaissance features with the English colonial style. Twice a week a colorful flea market takes place on the Grand Parade, the big square in front of City Hall.

2–18 Harare Market, Harare, Zimbabwe
A traditional market in an urban context of modern architecture invites tourists and locals to enjoy local produce and products

'On the same day that one can see the desert and the sea, it is also possible to see mountains and forests. These contrasts of nature are indigenous to the Mediterranean countries and the Middle East and have produced markedly different modes of living and culture. A maritime civilization evolves from the sea opening to the outside world. Mountainous regions, by contrast, are much more difficult to access. The plain, flat country ripe for agriculture is inhabited by long-standing cultures of farming communities. There is also the desert, a geography on maps and geography for the imagination, in particular, the western one. Its African character is suggestive of various commercial exchanges in the past between different tribes and African regions.' (From Ahmed Radi, *Hybridity and the Strategies of Instability*, Morocco, 2001)

Architectural illustrations that possess clarity and precision originate with the visualization of environments in concert with the sensitive representation of culture and context. The Mediterranean and Middle East cartographies are as varied as any in the world, making the architectural illustration as provocative in geographic context as it is visionary in design. A provocative illustration is distinguished by one essential element—its concept that springs from a plan and also from an abstract pattern of light and form based on an understanding of the subject and its geographic and cultural context.

From the oldest civilizations of the Mediterranean to the cradle of civilization in the Middle East, new city centers and urban redevelopments are transforming this area of the world into a dynamic blend of age-old civilizations, and modern versus nomadic cultures.

Vigorous forms of migration, mobility, and intermarriage within these cultures, countries, and nation-states make for a mixture of regional density where melting pots are shaped and reshaped. There are also emerging cities that strive to integrate modernity into a rural lifestyle, and by doing so create a hybrid population in search of a better way of life and more complex identity, struggling to come to terms with globalization.

The challenge of creating representations of reality in context with a region includes accurate representation of the urban space and architecture, and the organization of surroundings that reflect natural relationships. The illustrations of public spaces in this region of the world are associated with many cultural cues. Public spaces in the Mediterranean and Middle East countries exist in many forms—squares, gardens, roads, avenues, parks and boulevards. Today, it is appropriate to add cafés, markets, shopping malls, government buildings and city centers. Public space is the sphere of the *polis*—an empty space open to everyone—and therefore accessible to all and contrary to private space.

3–1 Midan Tahrir Square, Alexandria, Egypt
Popularly known as 'Manphiya', it features an equestrian statue of Mohammed Ali, erected in 1873. The large square has no traffic lights—people cross wherever and whenever they can.

A 'public space' is a concept that can be defined quite differently by various disciplinary fields, especially political science and geography. The term has many layers of meaning, including a shared place, a particular type of architecture, a space for collective use, a place for public debate, and the cultural connotation perceived through images and the representations produced by the society from which they originate.

The Mediterranean and Middle East countries share intimately in a multiplicity of meanings, uses, purposes and ideas of public space. Perhaps a global definition would infer that a space or a place is a material object in continuous construction and therefore subject to modes of access through entrances, passageways, tunnels, and doors. Midan Tahrir Square, Alexandria, Egypt provides a grand plaza and welcome to visitors from around the world who come to Egypt to explore the secrets of the pyramids and the cradle of civilization (Figure 3–1). American University in Cairo showcases the integration of design form in Egyptian culture with modern architectural philosophy as a celebration of the vision for a campus and the future education of a new generation of Egyptians (Figures 3–2 to 3–4).

The popular image of the Middle East as predominantly desert and austere in character is overturned with a visit to any of the capital cities or major urban centers in the region. Laleh Park, in Tehran, Iran exemplifies the quality of green space throughout the capital city as well as the priority that Iranians place on the quality of environmental issues (Figure 3–5). Perhaps nowhere as dramatically as in Israel can one find architecture dating to the earliest moments and events of civilization. Monuments to the many religions and cultures have found a home nearby in the old city, and in the new suburbs and settlement towns of the Middle East (Figures 3–6 to 3–8). The markets are filled with the high pitch of rhetoric and frenetic activity—Jews, Arabs, Christians, Muslims, and others—engaged in selling produce, discussing politics, bartering between themselves, and of course selling product to tourists (Figures 3–11, 3–12).

In Fes, Morocco, the market is an alluring assemblage of centuries-old architecture—like a stage set for *Raiders of the Lost Ark*—intriguing and poised to enter the 21st century (Figure 3–10). Investment in commercial development in the Middle East is on the rise. Numerous projects such as Dubai mixed-use hotel developments, in Dubai, United Arab Emirates build upon the influx of international business investment (Figures 3–13, 3–14). The countries and cultures of the Mediterranean and Middle East, responsible for the development of philosophy, science, and building, pursue a growing cosmopolitan community of universities, businesses, recreational facilities, government buildings, resorts and sporting facilities. The nations of the Mediterranean and Middle East are rising to the challenge of retaining the customs and traditions of their culture while stepping into the dynamic new set of values associated with modern urban lifestyles and environments.

3–2 American University, Cairo, Egypt
The University Library, located in the heart of Cairo, is a modern design integrated with motifs from Egyptian culture
Hardy Holzman Pfeiffer Associates (HHPA)

3–3 American University, Cairo, Egypt
Hardy Holzman Pfeiffer Associates (HHPA)

3–4 American University Cairo, Egypt
Outdoor corridor at entry lounge
Hardy Holzman Pfeiffer Associates (HHPA)

3–5 Laleh Park, Tehran, Iran
Laleh park, located in the city center, is surrounded by hotels and museums, and takes its name
from the Farsi word for tulip, the flower having its origin in ancient Persia, now modern Iran

3–6 Street to Land Gate, Akko, Israel
The five-year plan for the redevelopment of Akko includes rehabilitation and restoration of the sites of historical and artistic value, development of infrastructure, encouragement and restoration of traditional arts and crafts, and the improvement of quality of life for the local population

3–7 Old Jaffa, Jaffa, Israel
Old Jaffa is filled with artists' quarters, studios, art galleries, and shops catering for Judaica, archaeology, jewelry, and art, all lining its narrow alleys which are named after the signs of the Zodiac

3–8 Damascus Gate, Jerusalem, Israel
Built by Suleiman the Magnificent in 1541, this is the most massive and ornate of Jerusalem's gates. Modern excavations show this to be the site of the main gate into the ancient city, the road from which leads to Shechem (Nablus) and on to Damascus. Today, it is an Arab street market for produce and money-changers.

3–9 Office tower and hotel, Beirut, Lebanon
Study sketch with harbor scene
Skidmore, Owings & Merrill (London)

108

3–12 Grand Bazaar, Istanbul, Turkey
Known locally as 'Kapali Carsi', this internationally known market place was originally built in 1461 by Sultan Mehmed the Conqueror. The current structure was built in 1898, after an earthquake destroyed the original buildings. Renovations followed fires in 1943 and 1954. Today, more than 3500 shops employ some 20,000 people.

Opposite top: 3–10 Fes Market, Fes, Morocco
Because of its proximity to the Sahara Desert, the crowded market streets of Fes are covered against the sun's intense glare and heat

Opposite bottom: 3–11 Old Jeddah, Jeddah, Saudi Arabia
Jeddah is a commercial and port city on the Red Sea. It has always been the commercial capital of the Kingdom of Saudi Arabia. Its significance does not come in the least from the fact that it has always been the key gateway for Muslim pilgrims traveling to the holy city of Makkah on pilgrimage (Haj or Umrah), while also being on the crossroads of age-old caravan trading routes.

Opposite: 3–13 Dubai Mixed-Use Development, Proposed Mixed-Use Projects, Dubai, United Arab Emirates
Numerous projects, which have been announced recently, are designed to place Dubai among the top destinations for business and holiday travelers. Dubai is on the path
to become the cynosure of the world's eyes. Massive and trend-setting projects have been launched by the emirate, in its bid to be a world-class tourist destination.
WBTL Architects

ASIA–PACIFIC EMERGENCE

A mastery of graphic instrumentation and effective communication design are the hallmarks of the architectural delineator who possesses the ability to find the essential perspective view that provides the most comprehensive orientation for depicting space. Despite the similarities of modern architectural design, especially the high-rise glass-and-steel towers of the late-20th century, there are certain differences among them, such as visual elements and existing contexts, that are extremely important to the depiction of future urban spaces and the completion of the architect's vision.

Some of the largest and most ambitious urban planning and design projects today are being constructed in Asia–Pacific countries. These projects stem from the sweeping changes in a global economy and a new perspective to engage in an international dialogue regarding foreign trade and global culture. Although countries around the world are eager to participate in a global economy, perhaps none are as ambitious and as large in scale as those currently in design and under construction in Asia.

High-density environments in the Asia–Pacific region are characterized, in part, by gleaming towers as symbols of globalization and technological expansion. The Petronas Towers, in Kuala Lumpur, Malaysia, designed by Cesar Pelli, signaled a new boom in the design and construction of the world's largest structures. The illustrations for these new urban centers portray the existing context rendered either as the realization of the architecture in context with the urban space, or often as a proposal for further professional study and modification.

The emergence of contemporary society in the Asia–Pacific region is dominated by the globalization of markets and culture and by the associated dilemmas of sustainable development and environmental pollution. Nevertheless, numerous projects such as the Bionic Tower, Hong Kong; Shanghai World Financial Center, Shanghai, China; and the Taipei Financial Center, Taipei, Taiwan are all on the drawing board and several are under construction.

The growing interaction between urbanization and globalization will signal the advent of an urban century and the heightened role of cities in the growth of world population. Breathtaking transformations in technology, often referred to as an 'information revolution,' include computer, electronics, robotics and telecommunications, and are at the forefront of new research along with material science and biotechnology. Revolutionizing business transactions and encouraging creativity, architects are planning urban cities for a revolution in the way we communicate, work, and enjoy recreation.

A high-density environment has been one of the salient features of recent Asia–Pacific urbanization. Perhaps this is the result of economic necessity rather than a deliberate decision. However, the goal of designing urban spaces with vibrant architecture and the characteristics of sophisticated modern life points to the fundamental necessity of sustaining quality of life with spatial and technological sophistication. New forms of human habitation are being introduced that shift away from the modern paradigms that shaped Asia–Pacific cities during the 20th century.

Regional and urban centers have increased the amount of development on waterways, necessitating urban management. In Australia, the management of natural resources by industry, government, designers and planners is a main concern as to the quality of life and opportunities for change and innovation. Melbourne's reputation as 'one of the world's most livable cities', and Perth's great cultural diversity and proximity to Asia, reflect master plan projects that are preparing the cities for the future. Included in these projects are the development of fringe areas, transportation, areas of great natural resources and beauty, gateways, riversides, and strong commercial cores (Figures 4–1, 4–2). Sydney, Australia, home to one of the world's most magnificent waterfronts, is witnessing new high-rise residential developments whose aesthetic and environmental qualities are being fiercely debated by local communities, politicians, developers and architects (Figures 4–3 to 4–5). Australia's major cities are positioning themselves for new infrastructure projects, including CityLink transportation, expansion of cultural districts, exhibition centers and waterfront venues, development of parks and sports facilities, high-density housing projects, and heavy rail transportation initiatives.

Symptomatic of real worldwide problems, Australian cities face problems of growth in infrastructure, transportation, government, and pocketed real estate investment. It could also be said that an increase in problems of air pollution and water quality are being experienced and monitored. Car dependency, however, remains one of the largest problems in Australian cities. Just as in North America and other countries throughout the world, integrated planning is being called for in Australia, including land use such as the urban–rural fringe, transport, social services, environment, and all levels of government.

In Beijing, China, the government has allocated a staggering sum of money—over US$102 billion—for construction projects over the next five years, and much of this is to be spent on sporting venues, public design projects and transportation infrastructure. There is no doubt that, particularly in the field of design, engineering, planning and management, the Chinese need support from the international construction industry for such a huge venture in the run-up to the 2008 Olympic Games.

The relatively recent Beijing Entertainment Complex by Skidmore, Owings & Merrill reflects the commercialization of architecture in order to attract business investment and tourism (Figure 4–6). The exteriors of many commercial projects are often adorned with banners and advertisements. The emphasis on urban density is strong, but planners in Asian countries are making successful efforts to retain traditional attributes by incorporating parks, gardens, plazas, and green spaces in new developments. The renderings of Lishan Plaza (Figures 4–7, 4–8), Hong Kong Park (Figure 4–9) and Orchard Street (Figure 4–20), Singapore all demonstrate contemporary urban centers with modern and historic buildings, ample green space, and the integration of public parks and plazas as sanctuary from city life.

The growth of economies in the Pacific Rim prior to the recent economic crisis was a main factor of national economic policies that fortified the growth of urban policy infrastructure and sweeping new changes in urban design and community building. The cityscapes of Asia are undergoing great change and transformation. With the loss of traditional neighborhoods and the substitution of the conventional urban fabric with faceless modern cities, the significance of good neighborhoods and livable urban spaces that provide a productive setting for a healthy urban life are increasingly being acknowledged.

The knowledge-intensive, new techno-economic paradigm has arrived in Asia, as it has around the world. This has brought with it a new borderless economy as the cornerstone of the 21st century, fostering a functional urban system with world cities playing various key roles in a global society interdependent on systems of finance, transportation, telecommunications, services, and production.

The production of new urban spaces has lead to the realization of many contemporary urban mega-projects in Pacific Rim cities and elsewhere. These 21st-century urban enclaves are the realization of international corporations' investment in the processes of cultural interconnections, linkages, and interdependencies. After two millennia of development, the trend of globalization and integration will unfold in an urban century. Economic production, social organization and knowledge generation will be the city of the future. Citizens will be prone to 'think globally and act locally'.

In a lecture paper given to the First Biennial Conference of the Urban History Association in September 2002, Robert Fishman of The Taubman College of Architecture and Planning, The University of Michigan, relates the following provocative true story regarding the developing urban fringe. 'In 2002, a story in *The Los Angeles Times* reported the opening of a new US$60-million gated community of 143 condominium units (US$250,000 to US $1million) or tract mansions designed by California architect Aram Bassenian. Visitors dined on McDonald's cheeseburgers as they toured the upscale suburban designs, including open floor plans, cathedral ceilings, and custom kitchens. Advertised as Pure American, the units sold quickly. What makes this development unusual is that it is located in the suburbs of Beijing close to the site of the 2008 Summer Olympics and goes by the name, Orange County, China'.

Singapore, Shanghai, Pudong, and Jinhua, China are all witnessing massive transformation of their urban skylines with the revitalization of high-rise residential and office towers and construction of new city centers. Jinhua Plaza (Figure 4–10), Pudong Hospital (Figures 4–11, 4–12), Pudong Shanghai (Figures 4–13 to 4–15), and Sunjoy's Tomorrow Plaza (Figures 4–16, 4–17) exemplify the burst of a new and dramatic skyline in urban high-rise development projects. The architecture is symbolic of modern glass and steel construction, an economy of building for residential and office design (Figures 4–18, 4–19).

Malaysia, Indonesia, Thailand, and the Philippines are characterized by larger rural sectors than Singapore but are experiencing high rates of economic growth, from 7–9 percent per annum. As a result, infrastructure development is unable to cope fully with economic development and investment pressures. In Jakarta, Indonesia, one of the world's tallest buildings has been constructed to provide a symbol of the country's recent economic growth (Figure 4–21). The Plaza Mega Kuningan project (Figures 4–22 to 4–24) and Surabaya Resort (Figures 4–25 to 4–27) provide new offices, shopping plazas and urban resort tracts, created to attract tourism and lure customers into new department stores, cafés, and boutiques.

Hibiya Park, Tokyo, Japan is a symbol of the traditional Japanese urban parks found inside and outside urban centers throughout the country. Lush in vegetation with ponds, these oases are found in many Japanese city centers and are indigenous to the lifestyle of modern Japan (Figure 4–30). Modern office complexes exemplified by Saitama Municipal and Government office buildings (Figures 4–28, 4–29) are being constructed in major cities throughout the country. In Japan as elsewhere in Asia, modern and efficient office park developments now ring major metropolitan centers at the fringe of suburbia.

One of the most populous cities in the Pacific Rim, Seoul, Korea, shows no sign of halting the march of urban density. New residential towers are continuously constructed as the city continues to develop commerce (Figures 4–31 to 4–35). Office towers, hotels, urban plazas and entertainment facilities (Figures 4–36 to 4–38) are being built throughout the region and reflect Asia–Pacific's emerging desire to participate fully in a global economy with emphasis on diversity across the board in production, services, and information sectors.

4–1 Southbank Park, Melbourne, Australia
Located on the Yarra River, the park features extensive walks and a children's water play area and seating from which to enjoy views of the skyline opposite

4–2 Kings Park Perth, Australia
Expansive urban garden spaces, such as Kings Park in Perth, provide dramatic views of the city

4–4 Sydney Harbour, Sydney, Australia
Skyline study sketch

4–3 Circular Quay, Sydney, Australia
'A major transport interchange of ferries, trains and buses, Circular Quay is located
in the "downtown" end of Sydney's central business district. Flanked by the Sydney
Harbour Bridge, Overseas Passenger Terminal and Sydney Opera House and with
spectacular north-facing views across Sydney Harbour, the Quay is always a vital and
active place for commuters and tourists alike' — Peter Stronach, Managing Director,
Allen Jack + Cottier, Sydney, Australia

4–5 Circular Quay, Sydney, Australia
Study sketch

4–6 Beijing Entertainment Complex, Beijing, China
Dazzling lighting and advertisements signify the Beijing Entertainment Complex as a business entity for international visitors
Skidmore, Owings & Merrill (New York)

4–7 Lishan Plaza, Beijing, China
Aerial view of Lishan Plaza, a mixed-use development and center point of Beijing real estate
Hellmuth, Obata + Kassabaum, Inc. (St. Louis)

4–8 Lishan Plaza, Beijing, China
Garden park planning for broad public spaces
Hellmuth, Obata + Kassabaum, Inc. (St. Louis)

4–9 Hong Kong Park, Hong Kong, China
A green area providing respite, surrounded by the skyscrapers of the financial district. The park features fountains and shaded seating areas.

4–10 Jinhua Plaza, Jinhua, China
A mixed-use development for business and residences
Lohan Associates

4–11 Pudong Hospital, Pudong New Area, Shanghai, China
The hospital is set back from street to provide a large public plaza with flower garden landscaping
Hellmuth, Obata + Kassabaum, Inc. (Los Angeles)

4–12 Pudong Hospital, Pudong New Area, Shanghai, China
Aerial study sketch

4–13 Pudong Shanghai Project, Shanghai, China
The futurist dream of a global and international city
includes cultural symbols from the past
Hellmuth, Obata + Kassabaum, Inc. (Los Angeles)

4–14 Pudong Shanghai, Shanghai, China
A mixed-use development
Hellmuth, Obata + Kassabaum, Inc. (Los Angeles)

Opposite: 4–15 Pudong Shanghai, Shanghai, China
A new business tower development with a waterfront interest
Hellmuth, Obata + Kassabaum, Inc. (Los Angeles)

4–16 Sunjoy's Tomorrow Plaza, Shanghai, China
The unique building profile sits adjacent to a public park and shopping center
Hellmuth, Obata + Kassabaum, Inc. (Santa Monica)

Opposite: 4–17 Sunjoy's Tomorrow Plaza, Shanghai, China
Business and residential spaces are integrated into a new urban complex
Hellmuth, Obata + Kassabaum, Inc. (Santa Monica)

4–18 HDB Singapore Project, Singapore
A new business tower with mixed-use office and residential space
Skidmore, Owings & Merrill (California)

4–19 HDB Singapore Project, Singapore
Entry view
Skidmore, Owings & Merrill (California)

4–20 Orchard Street, Singapore
The premier shopping street of Singapore, with wide pedestrian walks, extensive planting and seating areas

132

4–22 Kuningan Persade, Jakarta, Indonesia
Skidmore, Owings & Merrill (New York)

Opposite: 4–21 Proposed Office Tower, Jakarta, Indonesia
The noteworthy globe at the top of the building draws attention to its profile as an international business center
Skidmore, Owings & Merrill (New York)

4–23 Plaza Mega Kuningan Project, Jakarta, Indonesia
The office towers hover like a beacon, attracting attention to the
park-like setting for tourism and commercial spaces
PT Encona

Opposite: 4–24 Plaza Mega Kuningan Project, Jakarta, Indonesia
A new broad urban shopping plaza development at the base of a modern office tower
PT Encona

ROCHON

4–27 Surbaya, Surbaya, Indonesia
Hotel and residences
Hellmuth, Obata + Kassabaum, Inc. (Los Angeles)

Opposite top: 4–25 Surbaya, Surbaya, Indonesia
A hotel tower and residential suites with a golf course
Hellmuth, Obata + Kassabaum, Inc. (Los Angeles)

Opposite bottom: 4–26 Surbaya, Surbaya, Indonesia
A new resort development with recreation for all ages
Hellmuth, Obata + Kassabaum, Inc. (Los Angeles)

4–28 Saitama Municipal and Government Office Building, Saitama, Japan
These two towering structures seem well-suited to the suburban edge of Toyko where a terraced appearance is in keeping with the surrounding green spaces
Nikken Sekkei Architects

4–29 Saitama Municipal and Government Office Building, Saitama, Japan
Aerial study sketch
Nikken Sekkei Architects

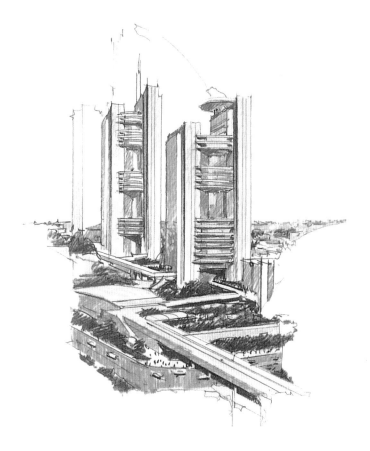

4–30 Hibiya Park, Tokyo, Japan
Built in 1903 in the 'modern' style of the day, it was the first western-style park in Japan and is surrounded by Tokyo's financial district

4–31 Suyoung Bay Arena, Pusan, South Korea
Public spaces adjacent to the arena are filled with eateries and tourist vendors
Skidmore, Owings & Merrill (New York)

4–32 Suyoung Bay Arena, Pusan, South Korea
Entertainment is a major attribute in a country that enjoys popular music
Skidmore, Owings & Merrill (New York)

4–33 City Department Store, Seoul, Korea
Spacious streets, broad pedestrian sidewalks and a dynamic modern architecture look forward to a positive impact on the city
Hellmuth, Obata + Kassabaum, Inc. (St Louis)

4–34 City Department Store, Seoul, Korea
Super graphics draw attention to the commercial shopping district
Hellmuth, Obata + Kassabaum, Inc. (St Louis)

4–35 Seoul Street Scene, Seoul, Korea
Seoul is one of the world's most densely populated cities, with over 15 million people. A construction boom begun
in the 1960s continues today, bringing the consequent urban problems of housing density and circulation.

4–36 Sultan Abdul Samad Building, Kuala Lumpur, Malaysia
Built by the British in 1897 for their government's administrative offices, it now houses the Supreme Court of Malaysia and a textile
museum of brick and exposed stucco. It is in the 'Mohamet' style, the Western interpretation of South Asian form and decoration.

4–37 Rockwell Center, Manila, Philippines
A dramatic office tower with a striking linear roof-top makes a strong impact on the austere island country
Skidmore, Owings & Merrill (Chicago)

4–38 Taipei Street Scene, Taipei, Taiwan
Taipei is a city of 25 million people that experienced rapid growth after World War II. In the older parts of town, narrow streets wind past many small, well-maintained shops and offices.

European Traditions

Architects and illustrators address the design of spaces that promote social encounters, indoor and outdoor public gatherings, and settings that support the community and public life. The great cities of Europe are models for the relationship of architecture to public space and for the meaningful arrangement of buildings and their use and function. European planners celebrate the architectural and social attributes of public spaces and recognize the important role of human interaction in everyday public life.

Many cities in history were designed with a sense of order and clarity, and a sensitivity to visual perception and patterning. The European medieval city, once the center of commerce, religion, and social life, was the focus of vital human experience including ceremonies, public functions, and celebrations. Europeans have for centuries preserved their city centers as cores of urban experience. The drama and tapestry of human events that occurs in town squares, church courtyards, gardens, public parks, and plazas have been preserved today as traffic-free zones that provide vibrancy to urban life and a flourishing of public experience.

Cities are composed of streets, boulevards, squares, parks, and buildings, all of which give form and structure to the city's public spaces. Each city has its own unique image and tradition, expressed through the character of those public spaces. European cities in the 20th century are dotted with contemporary projects in the urban landscape that extend the values of their architectural heritage to provide new vitality with life-affirming qualities for their inhabitants. In cities and towns throughout the continent, architects and planners are working together to design public spaces and civic projects. These projects, including public plazas, parks, waterways and fountains, architecture and the spaces between, help reinvest urban corridors with sensible qualities of human experience and greater sensitivity to human activity, circulation, and scale.

The physical attributes of public spaces endow the urban experience with life and liveliness. The architectural attributes of urban design are the focal points, boundaries, and territories for individuals or groups. They are viewed by the designer as street furnishings and include benches, seats, planters, walls, steps, fountains, tables, and chairs. More significantly, the theater of public space is similar to good stage design in that the props have been designed to create settings that are appropriate to the variety of personal, interpersonal, and group activities that take place there. Plazas belong to the people. Users vary during the course of the day from those who meet in the morning to talk and mingle, to midday tourists who congregate to view the sites, to evening visitors who return from work and recreation to see-and-be-seen. All derive pleasure from the cafés that adorn the sidewalks with bright umbrella tables and ornamentation.

Paul Klee said that the way we perceive form is the way we perceive the world, and nowhere is this more evident and beautifully displayed than in the sketching and drawing of the urban environment. The art of composition—bringing order to the various subject elements that make up the view of city life—is both intuitive and conscious. The arrangement of form in space and the illustrator's visual sense of design are important factors in laying out a subject for an illustration and resolving any problems that occur. In many instances, the center of interest in architectural illustration is a single building or group of buildings, an urban landscape, an interior view, and the people who inhabit the space. Making the main subject prominent but not overwhelming is an artistic problem with many aesthetic solutions.

In Stroget Street, Copenhagen, Denmark (Figure 5–1), the urban context and architecture are developed into pictorial composition with sensitivity to the elements that humanize public space and add an important dimension of subtlety to a composition. Posing people in the foreground of a busy urban plaza, combined with the architecture as a foil in the middle space and background, establishes a fitting and compelling degree of contrast of scale, and a tension between the period style of the architecture and the contemporary image of the whole picture.

The ability to capture the essential visual elements, including the mood, of an urban design scheme for an illustration is achieved through many attempts at simplification, resulting in maximum effect using minimum detail. One of the most important secrets is that even the most complicated structure has basic, underlying patterns of shape, form, color, and texture that, individually or together, can form a simple visual pattern and establish the theme for a single sketch or series of explorations. Examples of this are the drawings of Royal Crescent, Bath, England (Figures 5–2, 5–3), and Liverpool Docks (Figure 5–4).

The illustrations of 1 Ludgate Place (Figure 5–5), Canary Wharf, London, England (Figure 5–6), and 100 New Bridge Street (Figure 5–7), demonstrate a brevity of stroke along with concise definition of form and space, and reflect the intention of simplicity in illustration, and an economy of means, especially in pencil. These highly contemporary buildings designed by Skidmore, Owings & Merrill, are all established in the middle ground of their pictorial compositions allowing for the appreciation of their distinctive setting and urban landscape. The relation of the whole of the composition, as well as the relation of the subject and its size to other objects in the picture, is the main interest.

Paul Klee also said, 'Drawing is taking a pencil for a walk to see what it encounters along the way'. Such factors as value range, line weights, the use of background space, and the concise definition of form all contribute to a hierarchy of visual interest and are therefore important visual elements of drawing and design in the successful illustration of the content. Beyond the formal process of perception in sketching lies the dynamic activity of translating, interpreting, and storing information. In the sketches for Trafalgar Square (Figures 5–8, 5–9), the transformation of real images into drawn symbols involves identification, simplification, and expression. Sketching as a reflex action includes drawing what you see and what you know. Transporting the viewer into the activity of the site, however, requires a special empathy with the subject. In Trafalgar Square, the view of birds flying above the square transports the viewer of the illustration into a realm of physical movement and reality.

The movement in urban design to focus attention on natural subjects such as landscape, water, and people in public settings such as parks, markets, plazas and squares, has numerous advantages, especially in support of gaining acceptance for urban design projects. The market area adjacent to the main harbor in Helsinki, Finland (Figures 5–10, 5–11) is one of the most-recognized public spaces in the city. The background of government and university buildings and the Russian Orthodox church to the right acts as an elaborate stage for the daily human activity of buying fresh produce, seafood, and goods for the home.

The gardens and parks throughout Europe best capture the special qualities of public and private human experience in European urban life. In Paris, France, the Luxembourg Gardens (Figure 5–13), Palais Royal (Figure 5–14), Parc Montsouris (Figure 5–15), and Montmartre (Figure 5–16) all reflect the special character of intimacy in both formal and informal urban settings. The illustrations strive to capture the moment as one experiences it—a single frame of pictorial design with all of the important nuances of dappled light, color impression, human activity, and appropriate perspective viewpoints.

The role of the architectural illustration for design competitions in dense urban settings is to communicate an immediate impression of the building form within its intended environment. Aerial views of five architectural project competitions in Berlin, Germany, four by Skidmore, Owings & Merrill, and one by Lohan Associates (Figures 5–17 to 5–19), reflect the role of the vignette composition, or framing of the main architectural subject, by the use of simplification of detail in adjacent buildings and background contrasts in color and value. The competition illustration for the design of a new bank in Frankfurt, Germany for Skidmore, Owings & Merrill (Figure 5–21) demonstrates the importance of the illustrator's viewpoint in aiding the client's visualization, understanding and appreciation of the subject and its context within the larger fabric of architecture and urban setting. The glass-and-steel high-rise is viewed from a vantage point across the river, providing a realistic human scale and a clarity of spatial relationships of nearby buildings as well as an effective entrance viewpoint into the city.

Architecture as a stage set and the drama of public experience in urban space is nowhere better understood than throughout the city centers of Parma, Rome, Venice, and Verona, Italy. These illustrations (Figures 5–23 to 5–29) all demonstrate the spatial imagination and vision of public spaces and an architecture designed for both visual and monumental delight. The illustrations convey the romance of the architecture and a sense of the theatricality of the public space. The use of gatherings of people in daily activities, filling the squares and plazas in poses of walking, sitting, playing, and meeting, makes an immediate connection from the viewer to the urban space. The role of human activity in these drawings is an important illustrative device, directing the eye from the architecture to the spatial experience of the plaza and back to the architecture as a stage setting.

In the illustrations of Warsaw Center (Figure 5–31), Chiado Square (Figure 5–32), Arbat Street (Figure 5–33), St. Basil in Moscow (Figure 5–34), and the Royal Mile, Edinburgh, Scotland (Figure 5–36), the role of significant historic architectural form is given precedence and yet is woven into the continuity of the illustration through compositional orientation. These drawings convey the unique qualities of the urban illustration through the subtle manipulations of composition as well as interwoven contrasts in texture and color.

Arbat Street demonstrates a fascinating spatial viewpoint that showcases the balconies and architectural ornamentation of the apartment buildings at the ground level, viewing the rise of the façade into the sky. The illustration of St. Basil uses a careful application of warm (red) hues for the illustration of the onion domes and spires, and integrates this palette with earthier terra cotta tones at the base of the building and throughout the crowd of people that populate the plaza in front of the cathedral. Royal Mile in Edinburgh, Scotland showcases the façades of various period buildings along the streetscape through a demonstration of a perspective viewpoint looking down into the city. The role of color contrast between the terra cotta roof planes and spots of bright red elements in awnings,

automobiles and window shutters, promotes eye movement across the building façades without dominating the architectural interest of the scene.

Throughout the history of architectural illustration, the art of image-making has inspired and informed building. The interdependence of architectural design and illustration nourishes and informs each process. This book has included a demonstration of those principles and ideas of design communication—mass, volume, space, gesture, movement, context, and content, as well as atmosphere, color and light, shade and shadow, and intent and intonation.

Over the centuries of building and drawing, the architectural illustration as the predictive document and record of the design process has embodied the pure essence of the design, guiding and protecting the integrity of the architectural idea. The reflection of the city, building, or object captured in the lucid image of the architectural illustration has the unique capacity to convey multiple scales simultaneously, as it often represents the ideal point of view. It is a powerful visual communication tool, and is still the most persuasive and effective instrument to convey the essence of the art of building.

5–1 Stroget Street, Copenhagen, Demark
Copenhagen's old main street became its first car-free street. It is now the central artery of the city's pedestrian mall.

5–2 Royal Crescent, Bath, England
'Varying façades as a continuous unified architectural cornice to a park, private and public counterpoint, memorable sense of place' — Charles Gwathmey, FAIA, Gwathmey Siegel & Associates Architects

5–3 Royal Crescent, Bath, England
Study sketch

5–4 Liverpool Docks, Liverpool, England
'Art, music, food, people, history and a gritty robust architectural setting' — James S. Jones, Head, Department of Architecture, Kansas State University

5–5 1 Ludgate Place, London, England
A glass office tower, reminiscent of a trellis with climbing vines, has a spacious garden court
Skidmore, Owings & Merrill (London)

Opposite: 5–6 Canary Wharf, London, England
A new and dramatic commercial center planned for the eastern segment of Canary Wharf in London, England provides a river promenade as a key public element that links all parcels together and creates a backdrop for individual buildings
Skidmore, Owings & Merrill (New York)

5–7 100 New Bridge Street, London, England
A façade of layered forms and bright street-level storefronts create a unified context with a London business neighborhood
Skidmore, Owings & Merrill (London)

5–8 Trafalgar Square, London, England
*'The square has a wonderful architectural backdrop with the National Museum,
St. Martin in the Fields, and Naval Arch. It is heavily used by both pedestrian
and vehicular traffic, both of which seem to function without difficulty.'* —
Leslie H. Kenyon, Kenyon and Associates, Architects

5–9 Trafalgar Square, London, England
Aerial study sketch

5–10 Market Square, Helsinki, Finland
'The busy market square, with its orange stalls and appetizing smells that act as a magnet for shoppers, lies between the sea and the impressive row of historical buildings. Facing out to the sea are Helsinki City Hall, the Swedish Embassy, the Presidential Palace, and rising above in the background is the Russian Orthodox Church.' — Heikki Hirvonen

5–11 Market Square, Helsinki, Finland
Aerial study sketch

5–12 Dijon Opera House Competition, Dijon, France
The soaring elliptical lobby and varied forms of the new multipurpose Dijon Auditorium are illuminated from within against the fading light.
The auditorium is part of a modern exhibition and business center on the edge of Dijon, a small French town dating back to the middle ages.
Arquitectonica

5–13 Luxembourg Gardens, Paris, France
'The focus here is on human activities, from viewing displays of large photographs on the perimeter, to model sailboats in front of the Palais de Luxembourg, to the paths, sculpture and the versatility of movable chairs. Behavior settings are recorded at the end of the day by the seating configurations.' — Neville H. Clouten, Dean, Lawrence Technological University

Opposite top: 5–14 Palais Royal, Paris, France
'Layered landscape, arcade as extension and covered circulation. Sense of calm and multiple variations within an architectural frame.' — Charles Gwathmey, FAIA, Gwathmey Siegel & Associates Architects

Opposite bottom: 5–15 Parc Montsouris, Paris, France
The view from above the park hillside presents a picture-postcard respite from the bustle of city life and busy streets below. Opposite Cite' University, Parc Montsouris was designed in the English Style by the famous city planner Haussmann in 1868, with an artificial lake. The tranquility of the park and its surroundings attracts students, artists, elders, and mothers with babies to lounge on sunny lawns and stroll under the canopy of mature trees.

5–16 Montmartre, Paris, France
Montmartre is the highest hill of Paris and retains a very subtle and unique atmosphere in spite of the affluence of tourists from all over the world

5–17 American Business Center at Checkpoint Charlie Competition, Berlin, Germany
As a submission for a Berlin competition, the architect's design presents a dramatic organization of building forms, suggestive of a gateway or crossing
Skidmore, Owings & Merrill (New York)

5–18 Government Development, Berlin, Germany
The curvilinear façades circumscribe an interior campus-like courtyard and draw attention to the entrance
Lohan Associates

5–19 Berlin Competition, Berlin, Germany
The prevalent use of transparent building materials gives this architectural concept, an airy, open quality
Skidmore, Owings & Merrill (New York)

5–20 Central Square, Frankfurt, Germany
Scenic central square, the main shopping hub

5–21 DG Bank Competition, Frankfurt, Germany
This view across the river captures the prominent bank tower in its urban context
Skidmore, Owings & Merrill (New York)

5–22 O'Connell Street, Dublin, Ireland
The main street in Dublin, extensively damaged in a 1916 uprising, also suffered decay in the 1960s,
but is currently undergoing extensive redevelopment under architect Horace O'Rourke

5–23 Parma Street Scene, Parma, Italy

Parma, a car-free city rich in cultural history and gastronomic fare, swaddles pedestrians, allowing them to feel comfortable as they shop and socialize

5–24 Piazza della Rotunda, Rome, Italy
This piazza in front of the Pantheon was built by Pope Clement XI in the early 18th century and features an obelisk of Ramses II from Heliopolis

5–25 Piazza del Campidoglio, Rome, Italy

'Anticipatory, arrival, façade space enframing, sense of place, integration of sculpture.' — Charles Gwathmey, FAIA, Gwathmey Siegel & Associates Architects
Built on Capitoline Hill, an ancient Roman sacred site, the piazza was designed by Michelangelo to reflect Eternal Truth, spilling down the hillside as Goodness and Beauty into the secular city.

5–26 Piazza del Campidoglio, Rome, Italy
Study sketch

5–27 Santa Maria della Salute, Venice, Italy
'An intimate space despite its setting on the Grand Canal and the looming presence of the Santa Maria della Salute. What is so attractive to me is its powerful sense of place—once the pivotal point in a world economy dominated by Venice's merchant fleets.' — Paul L. Knox, Dean, Virginia Polytechnic Institute and State University

Opposite top: 5–28 Piazza San Marco, Venice, Italy
'It is the most beautifully proportioned open urban space I know and it is free of cars. It is the best people-gathering place anywhere in the world.' — Cesar Pelli, Cesar Pelli & Associates Architects

Opposite bottom: 5–29 Piazza delle Erbe, Verona, Italy
'At scale with the surrounding streets that lead to it, this piazza retains the vitality for which it was designed. It is a natural crossroads for pedestrian traffic and the beat of its fruit and vegetable market echoes both the daily tempo of the city and the seasonality of the region.' — Paul L. Knox, Dean, Virginia Polytechnic and State University

5–30 Main Market Square, Krakow, Poland

'The market square is at the heart of the old city, with Gothic and Renaissance façades to the Church of Our Lady and the Draper's Hall. As a center for human activities, the urban space reaches back into history when Krakow was the capital of Poland. City-dwellers and visitors follow the sequence from the flower stalls to the wooden triptych of the Blessed Virgin by Viet Stoss.' — Neville H. Clouten, Dean, College of Architecture and Design, Lawrence Technological University

5–31 Warsaw Center, Warsaw, Poland
Office building with first-floor retail in new urban redevelopment zone
Hellmuth, Obata + Kassabaum (HOK), Inc. (St. Louis)

5–32 Chiado Square, Lisbon, Portugal
A high-end shopping area in Baxia (lower town), the heart of Lisbon, filled with pedestrian streets, cafés and shops in a carefully preserved setting of centuries-old architecture

5–33 Arbat Street, Moscow, Russia
Lined with elegant old former diplomats' and ministers' mansions,
it was gentrified in the 1980s and features cafés and shops

Opposite: 5–34 St Basil's Cathedral, Moscow, Russia
The Jewel of Red Square, built 1555–1561 by Ivan the Terrible as a cluster of eight
churches surrounding one larger church, all on one foundation, each with a unique dome

5–35 Novgorod Hotel, Novgorod, Russia
New city plan with hotel and adjacent residential towers
Hellmuth, Obata + Kassabaum (HOK), Inc. (St. Louis)

5–36 Royal Mile, Edinburgh, Scotland
'Dramatic contrasts of historic periods of architecture, building forms and materials terrace down the hillside, providing a sumptuous parade of building materials and architectonic period forms' — Leslie H. Kenyon, Kenyon and Associates, Architects

LIST OF ILLUSTRATIONS

Illustrated by Richard Rochon

ARCHITECTS' COMMENTARY

SELECTED BIBLIOGRAPHY

Bacon, Edmund N, *Design of Cities*, Penguin Books, New York, 1974.

Bishop, Kirk R, *Designing Urban Corridors*, American Planning Association Planners Book Service, Chicago, 1989.

Calvino, Italo, *Invisible Cities*, Harcourt Inc, New York, 1974.

Cullen, Gordon, *Townscape*, Reinhold Publishing Corporation, New York, 1961.

Dixon, John Morris, *Urban Spaces*, Visual Reference Publications, New York, 1999.

Environmental Design Press, *How to Make Cities Liveable*, Van Nostrand Reinhold Company, New York, 1984.

Fishman, Robert, *Global Suburbs*, First Biennial Conference of the Urban History Association, Pittsburgh, Pennsylvania, September 2002.

Gapp, Paul, *The American City*, A Tribune Publication, Chicago 1981.

Gebhard, David, *200 Years of American Architectural Drawing*, Whitney Library of Design, New York, 1977.

Halprin, Lawrence, *Cities*, Reinhold Publishing Corporation, New York, 1963.

Hedman, Richard, *Fundamentals of Urban Design*, American Planning Association Planners Book Service, Chicago, 1985.

Katz, Peter, *The New Urbanism: Toward an Architecture of Community*, McGraw-Hill, New York, 1994.

Kamin, Blair, *Why Architecture Matters: Lessons from Chicago*, The University of Chicago Press, Chicago, 2001.

Kelbaugh, Doug, *The Pedestrian Pocket Book*, American Planning Association Planners Book Service, Chicago, 1989.

Lennard, Suzanne H Crowhurst, *Livable Cities Observed: A Source Book of Images and Ideas*, Gondolier Press, Carmel, 1995.

———, *Public Life in Urban Spaces: Social and Architectural Characteristics Conducive to Public Life in European Cities*, Gondolier Press, Carmel, 1984.

Linton, Harold, *Color in Architecture: Design Methods for Buildings, Interiors, and Urban Spaces*, McGraw-Hill, New York, 1999.

———, *Sketching the Concept: Perspective Illustration for Architects, Designers, and Artists*, Design Press, New York, 1993.

Lynch, Kevin, *A Theory of Good City Form*, MIT Press, Cambridge, Massachusetts, 1982.

Magnago Lampugnani, Vittorio, *Architecture of the 20th Century in Drawings: Utopia and Reality*, Rizzoli International Publications, Inc., New York, 1982.

Marshall, Richard A, *Emerging Urbanity—Global Urban Projects in the Asia Pacific Rim*, Spon Press, London, 2002.

Miao, Pu, Ed., 'Public Places in Asia Pacific Cities: Current Issues and Strategies', *Geojournal Library*, Vol 60, Kluwer Academic Publishers

Mumford, Lewis, *The Culture of Cities*, Harcourt Brace, New York, 1938.

Nakamura, Toshio, *Architecture and Urbanism: David M. Childs/SOM, 1976–1993*, a+ u Publishing Co., Ltd., Tokyo, 1993.

Radi, Ahmed, *Hybridity and the Strategies of Instability*, Political Discourse and Theories of Colonialism and Post-Colonialism, Casablanca, Morocco, 2001.

Rochon, Richard and Harold Linton, *Color in Architectural Illustration*, Van Nostrand Reinhold, New York, 1989.

Stamp, Gavin, *The Great Perspectivists*, Rizzoli International Publications, Inc., New York, 1982.

Swirnoff, Lois. *The Color of Cities: An International Perspective*, McGraw-Hill, New York, 2000.

Whyte, William H, *The Social Life of Small Urban Spaces*, Edwards Brothers, Inc., Ann Arbor, 1980.

———, *City: Rediscovering the Center*, American Planning Association Planners Book Service, Chicago, 1989.

Williams, Roy H, *Accidental Magic*, Bard Press, New York, 2001.